DINOSAUR WORLD
Swift Thief
The Adventure of Velociraptor

Written by Michael Dahl

Illustrated by Jeff Yesh

Thanks to our advisers for their expertise, research, knowledge, and advice:

Brent H. Breithaupt, Director
Geological Museum, University of Wyoming
Laramie, Wyoming

Peter Dodson, Ph.D.
Professor of Earth and Environmental Sciences
University of Pennsylvania
Philadelphia, Pennsylvania

Susan Kesselring, M.A.
Literacy Educator
Rosemount-Apple Valley-Eagan (Minnesota) School District

PICTURE WINDOW BOOKS
Minneapolis, Minnesota

Managing Editor: Bob Temple
Creative Director: Terri Foley
Editors: Nadia Higgins, Brenda Haugen
Editorial Adviser: Andrea Cascardi
Copy Editor: Laurie Kahn
Designer: Nathan Gassman
Page production: Picture Window Books
The illustrations in this book were rendered digitally.

Picture Window Books
5115 Excelsior Boulevard
Suite 232
Minneapolis, MN 55416
1-877-845-8392
www.picturewindowbooks.com

Printed in the United States of America.

Library of Congress Cataloging-in-Publication Data
Dahl, Michael.
Swift thief : the adventure of velociraptor / written by Michael Dahl ;
illustrated by Jeff Yesh.
p. cm. — (Dinosaur world)
Summary: Explains how scientists learn about dinosaurs and what their
discoveries have revealed about Velociraptor.
Includes bibliographical references and index.
ISBN 1-4048-0138-3
1. Velociraptor Juvenile literature. [1. Velociraptor.
2.Dinosaurs.] I. Yesh, Jeff, 1971- ill. II. Title.
QE862.S3 D34 2004
567.912—dc21
                                                    2003004043

No humans lived during the time of the dinosaurs. No people heard them roar, saw their scales, or felt their feathers.

The giant creatures are gone, but their fossils, or remains, lie hidden in the earth. Dinosaur skulls, skeletons, and eggs have been buried in rock for millions of years.

All around the world, scientists dig up fossils and carefully study them. Bones show how tall the dinosaurs stood. Claws and teeth show how they grabbed and what they ate. Scientists compare fossils with the bodies of living creatures such as birds and reptiles, who are relatives of the dinosaurs. Every year, scientists learn more and more about the giants that have disappeared.

Studying fossils and figuring out how the dinosaurs lived is like putting together the pieces of a puzzle that is millions of years old.

This is what some of those pieces can tell us about the dinosaur known as Velociraptor.

A hot sun blazed down on a dry, windy plain. Velociraptor (vuh-LOH-suh-RAP-tuhr), a fierce meat-eating dinosaur, hid in the shadow of a pile of rocks.

Velociraptor stretched out her neck and peered at her prey. Several feet away, Protoceratops (PRO-toh-SEHR-uh-tops), a plant-eating dinosaur, nibbled on a clump of ferns. Protoceratops did not know Velociraptor was watching.

Velociraptor was one of the smallest dinosaurs but also one of the fastest. The dinosaur stood 3 feet (1 meter) high and weighed about 33 pounds (15 kilograms). Her fearsome meat-ripping jaws would have been level with a small child's head.

Velociraptor walked and ran on two feet. Some scientists believe Velociraptor could run up to 40 miles per hour (64 kilometers per hour). The little dinosaur could easily outrun larger creatures. Velociraptor's nickname is Swift Thief.

Velociraptor carefully stepped out from the rocks.
Her keen eyes blinked in the sunlight.

Most meat-eating dinosaurs,
such as Velociraptor, hunted on
two feet. Scientists call creatures
that walk on two feet bipeds.

Most dinosaurs had eyes on the sides of their heads. Velociraptor's eyes were pointed forward. This gave Velociraptor excellent vision for hunting. The dinosaur had a clear view of how far she stood from her prey.

Velociraptor's sharp claws clicked against the rocks. Protoceratops raised his head and turned toward the strange sound.

Velociraptor opened her jaws and rushed forward. Inside her large mouth were many sharp teeth. She used these to eat small dinosaurs and other animals.

Velociraptor had 54 teeth that slanted inward. The teeth helped Velociraptor grab her prey.

Protoceratops galloped down a steep, rocky trail. He kicked up clouds of dust and sand as he ran around large rocks. Velociraptor had strong legs. She easily hopped over the rocks as she closed in on her tasty target.

Velociraptor's long, stiff tail swung around as she stepped and strutted and hopped. The tail helped the dinosaur keep her balance as she raced after her prey and made quick turns.

Velociraptor's tail was more than 3 feet (1 meter) long.

The frightened Protoceratops stumbled on the path. The heavy creature slipped and fell. He rolled down a long slope of smooth sand.

Velociraptor stood at the edge of the trail. The hunter watched her prey far below. With a sudden push of her slim, muscular legs, Velociraptor jumped into the air and down the sandy slide.

Some scientists think Velociraptor may have been covered with feathers instead of scales. The feathers were too small to help the dinosaur fly, but they may have worked like a sail. They may have caught desert breezes and pushed the dinosaur as she ran.

The smaller, lighter Velociraptor raced toward her victim. She pounced onto the plant-eater's tough back.

Velociraptor's sharp, curving claws ripped through the larger dinosaur's scaly skin. The middle claws on Velociraptor's feet were between 3 and 4 inches (7½ and 10 centimeters) long.

Velociraptor's middle claws may have been retractable, like the claws on a cat's paw. They slid forward during an attack. Afterward, they slid back inside Velociraptor's toes.

Velociraptor slashed at her prey's throat
and belly with her feet. She gripped the head
of Protoceratops in her front claws. Protoceratops
roared with pain and crunched down on Velociraptor's
right arm. The small hunter could not escape.

Both creatures died in the hot desert. Sand blew across the plain,
burying the two bodies in a tangle of bones and blood.

In 1971, scientists uncovered the fossils of Velociraptor and Protoceratops in a Mongolian desert, north of China. The fossils were still locked in a fighting position.

The two skeletons were complete and not smashed. They had survived for more than 70 million years. As scientists study the dinosaur bones, they learn more and more about how the deadly Velociraptor looked, how she hunted, and how she died.

Velociraptor: Where ...

Velociraptor fossils have been found in Russia, Mongolia, and Montana.

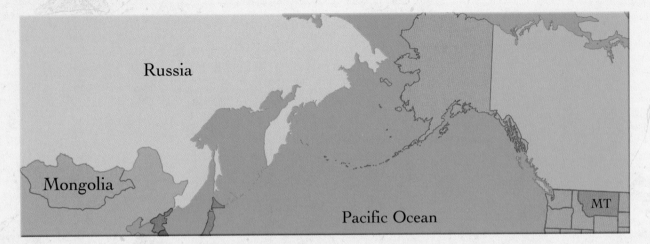

... and When

The "Age of Dinosaurs" began 248 million years ago (mya).
If we imagine the time from the beginning of the dinosaur age
to the present as one day, dinosaurs lived almost 18 hours—
and humans appeared just 10 minutes ago!

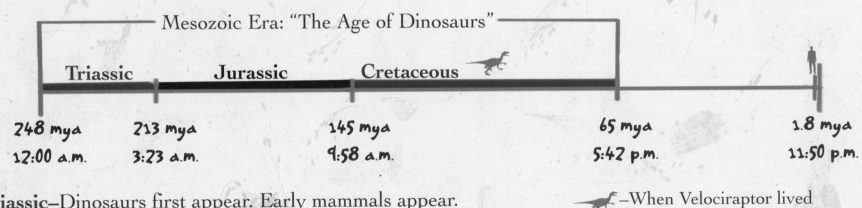

Triassic—Dinosaurs first appear. Early mammals appear.
Jurassic—First birds appear.
Cretaceous—Flowering plants appear. By the end of this era,
   all dinosaurs disappear.

—When Velociraptor lived

—First humans appear

Digging Deeper

Hunting in Packs

Velociraptor had a dangerous cousin named Deinonychus (dy-NOH-nih-kuhs). Scientists have found skeletons of a pack of Deinonychus that died while attacking another dinosaur. Some scientists think Velociraptors also may have hunted in packs of four or five.

Raised Toes?

Velociraptor's hook-like second toes were the dinosaur's best weapons. Some scientists think the toes' talons did not slide in and out like a cat's claws. They say the razor-sharp talons were always out. As it walked, Velociraptor raised these toes to keep them from scraping along the ground.

Handy Hands

Velociraptor had unusual hands for a dinosaur. Most dinosaur wrists only moved up and down. Velociraptor's hands also bent from side to side, like human hands. Velociraptor probably used its nimble hands for gripping its prey while it ate. The hands were also flexible weapons during an attack.

Movie Monsters

Velociraptors make scary villains in Steven Spielberg's movie *Jurassic Park*. But the movie versions are much bigger and smarter than the dinosaurs really were. Real Velociraptors probably stood only 2 or 3 feet (less than 1 meter) tall.

Words to Know

biped—a creature that walks on two feet

dinosaur—a land reptile that lived in prehistoric times. All dinosaurs died out millions of years ago.

fossil—the remains of a plant or animal that lived between thousands and millions of years ago

prey—an animal that is hunted by another animal

retractable—able to slide in and out

swift—fast

To Learn More

At the Library

Cohen, Daniel. *Velociraptor.* Mankato, Minn.: Bridgestone Books, 2001.

Landau, Elaine. *Velociraptor.* New York: Children's Press, 1999.

Lessem, Don. *Raptors! The Nastiest Dinosaurs.* Boston: Little, Brown, 1998.

Prelutsky, Jack. *Tyrannosaurus Was a Beast: Dinosaur Poems.* New York: Mulberry, 1993.

On the Web

Enchanted Learning: Zoom Dinosaurs

http://www.EnchantedLearning.com/subjects/dinosaurs

For information, games, and jokes about dinosaurs, fossils, and prehistoric life

The Natural History Museum, London: Dino Directory

http://flood.nhm.ac.uk/cgi-bin/dino

For an alphabetical database of information on the Age of Dinosaurs

University of California, Berkeley: Museum of Paleontology

http://www.ucmp.berkeley.edu/museum/k-12.html

Online exhibits, articles, activities, and resources for teachers and students

Fact Hound

Fact Hound offers a safe, fun way to find Web sites related to this book. All of the sites on Fact Hound have been researched by our staff.

http://www.facthound.com

1. Visit the Fact Hound home page.
2. Enter a search word related to this book, or type in this special code: 1404801383.
3. Click on the FETCH IT button.

Your trusty Fact Hound will fetch the best sites for you!